art

ACROSS the AGES

ANCIENT EGYPT

KELLY CAMPBELL HINSHAW

chronicle books · san francisco

To Steve: Thank you for your
eternal patience and support

Permission to use the following photographs is gratefully acknowledged:

Front cover and title page: © Scala/Art Resource, NY; page 3: © The Ancient Egypt Picture Library; page 4: © Thompson Webb, University of Wisconsin, Madison; page 5: © The Ancient Egypt Picture Library; page 6, top left: © Araldo De Luca; bottom left: © Scala/Art Resource, NY; right: © Werner Forman/Art Resource, NY; page 7, top right: © HIP/Art Resource, NY; top left: © Araldo De Luca; bottom left: The Metropolitan Museum of Art, photograph © 1978 The Metropolitan Museum of Art; bottom right: © Erich Lessing/Art Resource, NY; page 8: © Erich Lessing/Art Resource, NY; page 11: © Araldo De Luca; page 12: © Vanni/Art Resource, NY; page 13: © Araldo De Luca; page 14: © Scala/Art Resource, NY; page 15, top: © Bildarchiv Preussischer Kulturbesitz/Art Resource, NY; bottom: © Araldo De Luca; page 16: © Cheryl Simeone/UC Botanical Garden at Berkeley; page 17: © HIP/Art Resource, NY; page 18–19: © Werner Forman/Art Resource, NY; page 20: © Erich Lessing/Art Resource, NY; page 22–23: © The Metropolitan Museum of Art, photograph © 1978 The Metropolitan Museum of Art; page 24: The Metropolitan Museum of Art, Funds from Various Donors, 1886 (86.1.35), Image © The Metropolitan Museum of Art; page 25: The Metropolitan Museum of Art, Rogers Fund, 1925 (25.3.182), photograph © 1992 The Metropolitan Museum of Art; pages 26–27: © Araldo De Luca; page 28: © Araldo De Luca; page 30: © Jordan Husney; page 31: © Wagdy Rizk; page 32: © Araldo De Luca.

Book design by Tracy Sunrize Johnson and Kyle Spencer.
Typeset in Skia and Bembo.
Manufactured in China.

Library of Congress Cataloging-in-Publication Data
Hinshaw, Kelly Campbell.
Ancient Egypt / Kelly Campbell Hinshaw.
p. cm. — (Art across the ages)
ISBN-13: 978-0-8118-5669-0 (pbk.)
ISBN-10: 0-8118-5669-0 (pbk.)
ISBN-13: 978-0-8118-5668-3 (hardcover)
ISBN-10: 0-8118-5668-2 (hardcover)
1. Art, Egyptian—Juvenile literature. 2. Art, Ancient—Egypt—Juvenile literature. I. Title. II. Series.
N5350.C18 2007
709.32—dc22
2006016849

Distributed in Canada by Raincoast Books
9050 Shaughnessy Street, Vancouver, British Columbia V6P 6E5

10 9 8 7 6 5 4 3 2 1

Chronicle Books LLC
680 Second Street, San Francisco, California 94107

www.chroniclekids.com

A long, long time ago in North Africa, the ancient (AIN-shent) Egyptians (ee-JIP-shuns) made magical art.

This picture of a king and queen was painted on the back of a gold chair.
Can you find the chair in this book?

The land all around them was desert, so they lived along the Nile River.

This is how the Nile River looks today.

The river gave them everything they needed: fish to eat and water for growing food.

Egyptian art celebrated life on the Nile.

This wall painting shows Egyptians working in fields and praying.
Can you find the Nile River?

The Egyptians made many different
kinds of art.

jewelry

sculptures

paintings

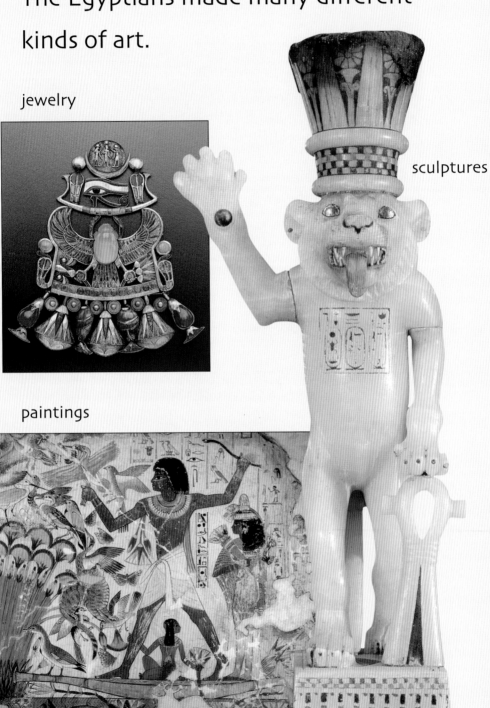

drawings

furniture

reliefs (pictures
carved in stone)

everyday things

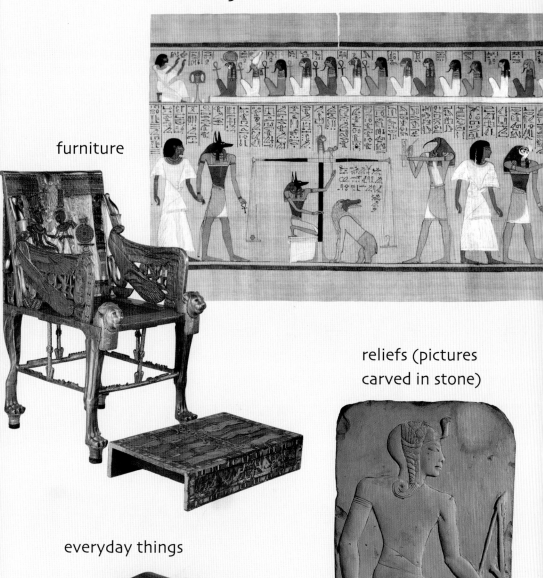

This sculpture is made of blue stone and gold.
It shows three gods: Isis (EYE-sis), Osiris (oh-SIGH-rus), and their son, Horus (HOR-us).

Ancient Egyptians believed that gods and goddesses ruled the world.

The people prayed to sculptures of these spirits.

Kings were called pharaohs
(FAIR-ohz) in ancient Egypt.
Egyptians believed the king
was both a person and a god.

This sculpture of a royal family
was carved from one huge
piece of stone.

The large size of the king and queen shows
their great power.

The princess is tiny—she does not have
much power.

Most sculptures were carved from stone then painted to look lifelike.

This is Queen Nefertiti (neh-fir-TEE-tee).

Her name means "beautiful" in Egyptian.

The best artists worked for the pharaoh and his family.

This pharaoh's throne is gold, the color of the sun.

Snakes and lions guard this throne. Can you find them?

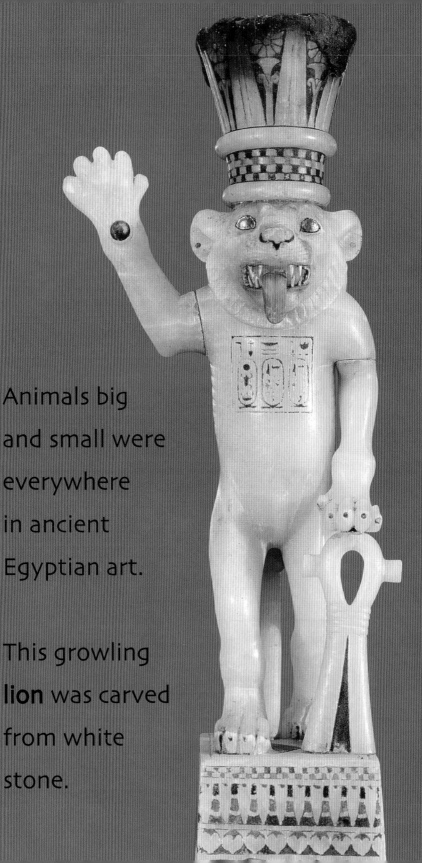

Animals big
and small were
everywhere
in ancient
Egyptian art.

This growling
lion was carved
from white
stone.

People wore
charms shaped
like **beetles**
for good luck.

This is a sculpture
of a **falcon** god.

Ancient Egyptians were the first
people to draw and paint on paper.
They made paper from papyrus
(puh-PIE-russ),
a plant that grows
along the Nile
River.

This is a page of papyrus from a book
of magical spells.

The words are hieroglyphs (HI-roe-glifs)—
Egyptian picture writing.

Large paintings covered the
walls of buildings in ancient
Egypt.

Most paints were made from
rocks.
Artists crushed the rocks into
powder and added liquid to
make paint.

Black paint was made from
burned wood or burned
bones.

In this wall painting a family hunts birds on the Nile.
Can you find their cat?

In this stone carving, a god fights a wild beast.
The god's face is very calm, like most faces in Egyptian art.

In ancient Egyptian art, heads
and bodies sometimes face sideways.
Shoulders face front.
This is uncomfortable—try it!
Egyptians thought people looked
better this way.

mirror

small jars for
eye paint

In ancient Egypt, simple things like
boxes and jars were also works of art.

shaving
tools

This makeup kit is made of wood.

All of the pieces fit neatly inside.

The Egyptians believed that after people died they went on to a new life.

The bodies of the dead were carefully wrapped in cloth.
Egyptians did this to make the bodies last forever.

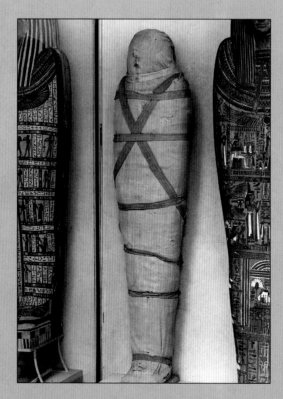

The wrapped bodies are called mummies.

Mummies were put in painted boxes.
The pictures were clues to help the mummies get to the next life.

There were dangers on the way to the next life.
Mummies wore special jewelry for protection.

The eye of the falcon god watched over the mummy.

This beetle had power from the sun god.

Cobra snakes scared off enemies.

Lotus flowers and papyrus brought new life.

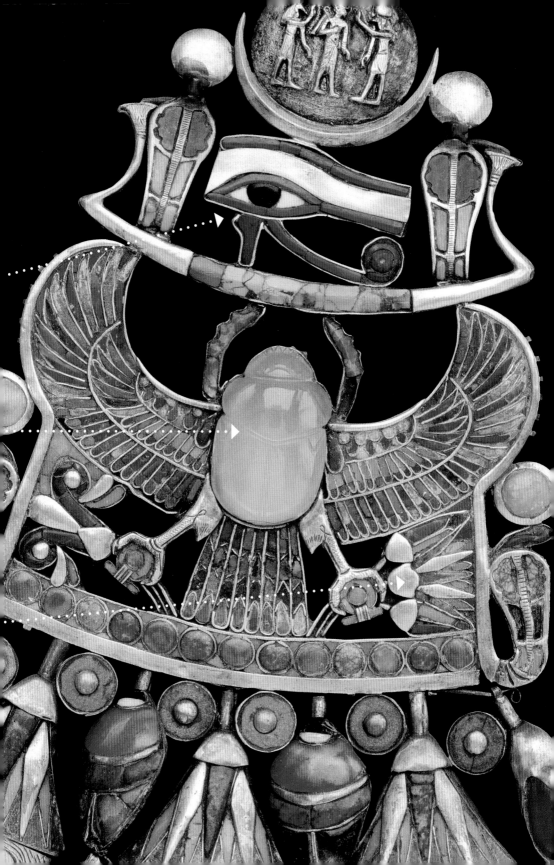

When pharaohs died, they were buried with furniture, clothes, and art: everything they needed for the next life.

This gold mask was found on the mummy of a young king.
You might know him as King Tut.

A pharaoh's mummy and treasures were hidden inside this great stone pyramid (PEER-a-mid).

Pyramids point up to the sun god in the sky.

Other Egyptians were buried in underground rooms, called tombs.

The paintings on tomb walls look like secret storybooks.

This is the tomb of a queen.

The ancient Egyptians lived more than 3,000 years ago.

A lot of their art was lost over time, but some was kept safe in tombs or buried under the sand.

Today you can see these treasures in museums around the world.

This is the Egyptian Museum in Cairo, Egypt.